double vision

Reese O'Connell

Edited by: Christian Lopez

ROYAL MEDIA
PUBLISHING

Royal Media and Publishing
P. O. BOX 4321
Jefferson, IN 47131
502-552-1643
www.royalmediaandpublishing.com
royalmediapublishing@gmail.com

© Copyright – 2020

All Rights Reserved. No part of this book may be reproduced, stored in a retrieval system, or transmitted by any means without the written permission of the author.

Cover Image: Brittany Baird
Cover Design: Elite Book Covers
Illustrations by: Reese O'Connell

ISBN: 978-0-9987154-9-0

Printed in the United States of America

Dedication

For the painfully misunderstood, the cynical bastards
& the wanderlusters.

For all those who are trying; even if it's a little bit.
This book is for you, dear reader.

Table of Contents

Dedication	iii
Coffee Shop Wonder	3
Temptation	7
White Walls	11
Eve	13
Lucid	15
Apathy	17
Sleep Paralysis	21
Jessie	25
Rocket Ship	29
Amanti	33
Fragmentation	37
X Chromosome	39
Insults	45
Nomad	50
Purple Storms	53
Golden Gate Bridge	55
Secrets	57
Rogue Planet	63
Empty Stage	65

Homesick	67
Valentine's Day	71
Voodoo Doll	75
Money	79
Transparency	83
Shooting Star	91
Dangerous	95
Karen	99
Astral	102
Glimpse	105
Damned	107
Fire in Water	109
Finish Line	111
Bermuda Triangle	117
God's Carousel	119
Millennials	125
That Boy	129
Visiting Hours: 3 AM	133
Jezebel	137
Bad at Love	141
Fixed	145
Hypocrite	153

Paradox	157
Bonnie & Clyde	161
Camillo	165
Y Chromosome	169
Manic Me	175
WWIII	179
About the Author	183

double vision

Coffee Shop Wonder

Wandering **this** city
in my world
that makes no sense,
cannonballs are crashing
in silence
I can only pretend.

The sky down
below me speaks
under the Bi-frost Bridge,

it **says** don't lose yourself
in the city limits
don't you ever quit.

Close my eyes
to **feel** the symphony
of the Cosmos
in my head,

dreaming of a time
when **reality**
made sense.

When did space
create time or
stars become our light,

where were you
as I tried to make
all this right?

The coffee I sip
sounds a little
more bitter,
sweet was a time
only when I was
with her.

The city lights
blind me in traces
of colour lines,
when did I forget
how to speak,
even then how to rhyme.

My world is not empty
don't get me wrong,
this confusion
of mine is insight
to those who belong.

My coffee
is getting cold.
How did I
get this old?

The more I try

to be sweet,

the more my

coffee gets

BOLD.

Temptation

It's the silence
before the chaos,
the sickening
disruption
before a quiet gunshot.

Whispering
whimpers
to a **painful** outcry,
asking me
to erase
if not distort time.

Heart beats racing
& dilated pupils,
to truly
yearn for something
authentically deceitful.

Doubled-edge

of sadistic temptation,

my body is wanting

a euphoric sensation.

Take one

for the pain

& one for the **party,**

you can take

off my clothes

& I won't even be sorry.

What is the hour

or even the day?

I'm breathing

the words

but forgetting

what to say.

Mix it

with rum &

come play

with my skin,

behind closed doors

we're all open to sin.

Cloud 10

will detach you

away from

your prison,

to leave

your **flesh** behind

is the humanly decision.

Sticks and stones

have broken my bones,

but your words

have crucified me

White Walls

This house

is empty

upon **my** arrival,

maybe it's me,

I'll blame the

long fucking miles.

These four walls

may project the **past**,

disheveled stories

displayed so fast.

In regard

to my manners

I **always** talk back,

for the ghostly riddles

I figure but

only see black.

So guilt me

my worst penalty

because I'm

your latest casualty,

I'm pretty much

everybody's favorite tragedy.

The **echoes**

here are intense & clear,

to shut it

all out &

forgive all my fears.

Where is a window

or even a door?

Give me some colour,

I can't

stand these white walls

Eve

Although **she**
was created
from Adam's rib,
we like to sit
around & blame her
for the first ever sin.

Her lack of wisdom
gave birth to knowledge,
that her skin was bare, &
the angel she spoke with
had fallen.

The charming serpent
whispered the deadly secret,
how she would not die
& the apple was meant
to be eaten.

How could she
know the difference of
truth & a lie?

If there'd been no other
obstacle in history
to help clarify.

She had no intention
of disobeying God,
she just did
what she was told &
now Earth is forever
flawed.

Imagine the guilt
when she learned
she was deceived,
after all,
God did put
the 'Eve' in **Naïve**.

Lucid

Meet me

in Dream-land,

I am tired

of the Waking World.

The people here

are too plastic,

the boring

& damned

all hidden

under foundation.

They make me **sick**.

I'm a mother

with no children.

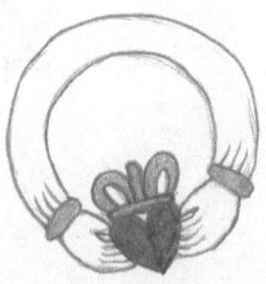

Apathy

Took the world in
but forgot myself,
inside the bed-sheets
of those to be felt.

With an invisible face &
luminous body,
they adore the person
I am only
when they're on me.

I'll wait for your call
as I reside in
this country,
believing if I don't
make it back
someone will come for me.

I'm lonely,
that stays for hours & minutes,
the rest of them
ask for more & yet I keep giving.

I can fit
inside the world
of an atom,
these particles
I attract are not
which I fathom.

I believe
there is light
when it's nowhere
in sight,
where were you
on the days?

I concluded **this**
loneliness **will**
proceed to make sense,
until your touch
on my skin
can **radiate** bliss.

Was Alice dreaming
or dead in her Wonderland?

Either way
behind her curiosity
I'll bet
she was sad.

If I can't sleep
am I
on **your** mind?

Or does magic
take place
as the **universe**
finds its align?

I'll continue
to empty myself
into your hands,
even after the blood
runs out of my heart's gash.

I've had every

kind of kiss,

but my favorite one

was when you

bit down so hard

you made my lip

start to bleed

Sleep Paralysis

It's **3 AM** &
I know
this eerie feeling,
how I'm awake
but my body's
still sleeping.

I can see my room
but my fingers
can't move,
this **is** the reason
I keep **my** night
lights blue.

I'm screaming
for help
inside my mind,

my limbs
are frozen & somehow,
I think
I've stopped time.

This sleep paralysis
has me
praying out
for help,
while that thing
at the end of my bed
stares at me
like he'd come
straight from Hell.

Every so often
he comes back
to watch me,
to strip away
the bravery

I have left
when I'm asleep.

I wish I knew
why this happens;
this **horror**
I have come to know,
I'm terrorized
these nights in bed
when I sleep alone.

When the shackles brake &
my body's finally free,
I regain my strength
to shout &
that monster finally flees.

One day

I hope

my heart

can love

the way

it hates.

Jessie

How far away
is Eden?
I'm sure you
found out in 2010.
You laid there
in your
uneventful casket,
& for the first time
I saw your face
without you laughing.

You were cold &
still which was nothing like you,
I can still hear
our sister scream
how she wanted
to go too.

The world was turned
upside down
at that unfaithful time,

the time you
flipped the car &
you were ejected outside.

She regrets
giving you those keys
that night,
I regret the things
I said
while we were
in that fight.

I'm **sorry**
that you were alone
while you were turning blue,
I was out
at that time partying &
getting a tattoo.

Ashley came
plunging in
through my room,

convulsed on the floor
while the paramedics
were holding you.

Her wailing
did not cease
night or day,
I was catatonic
with not a word to say.

I knew you were gone
when we set you into flames,
you visited at night &
told me you're ok.

I hear you
sometimes when you come around,
I'm sure it's not easy
watching all of us drown.

Please forgive me for
those nasty things I said,
know no matter
how I've hurt you,
its nothing compared
to the punishment
I've given myself for it.

October used to be
my favorite month,
I'll admit
sometimes it still is
kind of fun.

Thank you for helping me
stop blaming myself
for this tragedy,
I'll be good to you
in another life
away from this galaxy.

Rocket Ship

I yearn
to go home
I miss communication,
the quakes on Earth
are caused
by **separation**.

A planet
where man kills
his own brother,
one nation's greed
is another
country's hunger.

Plants are illegal &
animals go extinct,
we still deny
all the pain
we inflict.

We continue
to spread
the deadliest
virus today,
pretending as if
we don't have a cure
for this hate.

No we insist
the isolation
to stay,
melting us down
for all the light
to vacate.

Find me
in my backyard
from now on,
I'll be busy
building a rocket-ship
to God.

I don't want
to be
human anymore,
I'm scared
this **virus** will
find my core.

My depth
perception will be
clear from above,
we just need
to remember
that the cure is love.

The way that we treat
the material world says
a lot
about us.

Amanti

Saw you again

in **my** dream

last night,

you forgot

to tell me

what **Heaven** looks like.

More than a decade

in time

we haven't spoke,

you follow me

as I reach out

with an arm

that I broke.

I hate

to think of your body

but your ghost

is still fine,
did you think of
me once
when you left
the world behind?

Maybe you
haven't found
your way to the **light**,
you won't find
much chasing me
almost every night.

I'm sorry
for the things
I never said,
or how I should
have tried to be
a much better friend.

Find yourself
is all I can say
for now &
I'll leave you
with this my **love**,
I'll pray
every night
for Heaven to take
you up above.

Every step

I take

is a

poetic dance.

Fragmentation

I met **the devil**

one night

while I was praying,

for a new life,

begging for one

worth saving.

He grinned &

laughed

at my perseverance,

in Hell,

I guess you can

disguise your appearance.

We slow-danced

'til time

fell apart,

He snickered &

stated as always,

I took it too far.

Everyone else

was shocked

at the scene,

when I came back

the devil took

a big part of **me**.

X Chromosome

You said
you know
my heart,
because its
made from
your womb,
you said
you loved me,
I said
I loved you too.

Or maybe
you would cry,
just to have
me on your side,
being so little
I was **vulnerable**
to lies.

What stopped me
from living,

has now
given me a life.

Tell me
how to feel alive,
when the world
outside makes us
dead inside.

I'm swallowed
by fear,
unsettled by shame.

Guilted by far,
enraged by
hearing the sound
of your name.

The walls
of my cradle
are taller than you,
voices nearby
are everybody
but you.

In my cradle
my nights are so cold,
waiting for you
to get me
to hold.

The years go by
this cradle gets small,
by then
I learn myself
how to crawl.

How to get up
on my own
after each
one of my falls,
you still don't
pick up your phone
to call.

Years **fly** by
time makes
me older,
I'm wiser now &
very much colder.

My cradle still
rocks all by itself,
me, I'm the same.
I don't want any help.

Where were you
when my cradle got cold,
out getting your fix
is what I've been told.

Don't worry about me
I'll always be stable,
no one can hurt me
inside of my cradle.

You treat
me like a pinata,
but I still
hang right here
for you.

Insults

NOUN
insults (plural noun)
a disrespectful or scornfully abusive remark or action.

Insults are what seems
like a second language
currently in this world,
like throwing a punch
with your tongue,
someone always
ends up hurt.

I'm no stranger
to your negative implications,
instead, I find authenticity
in a bad reputation.

For instance,
that time
Mommy called me
a "whore"
with her microphone,

invited the whole town
to expose my sins &
she commanded they
throw their stones.

Reason was
that a boy
taught me how to kiss &
she sniffed
the story out,
what she didn't know,
is I was foolishly played
by a boy who only
likes to boast
to his crowd.

Or my boss
who claims
I just can't get along
with anybody,
even after
I made it clear
I'm just not high quality.

I'll admit,
I get into fights
nearly weekly,
the drunk man
at my bar
with expectations
just isn't easy for me.

I'll never forget
when a man I loved said,
"You'll end up like your mother
before you're dead."

I learned
quickly that day
just how mean
he could be,

I wish he knew addiction
is just as hereditary
as his perfect genes.

I've been called **a "slut"**
by a jealous little girl
in high school,
the boy she wanted
helped me
grieve my brother's death,
her envy grew.

She'd call me ugly **&**
stalked me for years
when I thought
I was a nobody.

Boys passed around
pictures of her 'kitty' &
laughed,
but I still think
she's prettier than me.

So now **I** can't wait
to see what you have to say
after familiarizing my moves,
it could make my day
or **destroy** my life;
it's up to you
to choose.

As there's two sides
to a story,
there's two sides
of an insult,
worst diss
I've had was from **myself**;
believing you all
with your mouths full.

Nomad

Here **I** go again
packing my bags,
leaving this town,
I **promise**
to not come back.

From racing thoughts
to losing my mind,
I ask this
be the final time.

This road I've driven
a thousand times,
a road with no exits,
the one with no lines.

I'll leave behind
our stories;
they won't be told,
my name will linger
in the air as it has before.

Forgive me
I do not learn,
I run in circles,
no one dares
straighten the life
of this girl.

This chaos
confuses
as well as consumes,
it rips apart reality
'til I get back to you.

As the times
here it
passes too slow,
the battle
in my head
only seems to grow.

The sound
I savor is
but bittersweet,

her voice
I hear again
after this last **retreat**.

Purple Storms

I've waited forever &

bared every storm,

patiently watched &

all **failed** to perform.

This storm

I ask for

is like no other,

I've met **them** all

just one after another.

I see my faith

getting hard to sustain,

hope the beauty

you vail puts

you to shame.

I'm always thinking

of you

there's no restrain,
but waiting
for you
is like waiting
for purple rain.

Golden Gate Bridge

I'll grab my things &
tonight leave this town,
no one to stop me
or concerns
of my whereabouts.

Maybe **I** will head
for San Francisco
to wait on the bridge,
dance with the jumping ghosts &
we'll mate in the mist.

Watch the city lights
from where I will sit,
unfortunate people
no where to be found
I see no conflict.

The fortune telling
bridge as my only support,
humanity is insane &
no longer what I yearn for.

The river below
counts the bodies un-souled,
I empathize
the presence of
their stories once told.

Loneliness drives
us to particular realms,
since you left
my heaven
has become like hell.

When the sky ignites
in big clouds of fire,
I slip from the bridge
to fall free
from these liars.

Secrets

I don't have a clue
how to deal
with my own antics,
so **I'll** list my flaws
without being too drastic.

I have unnatural eating habits
& leave the remote
in the fridge,
if I don't **get** 11 hours of sleep,
I turn into such a bitch.

I don't like to be
on the right
& hate touching doors,
I'll never listen to you
when I'm feeling bored.

I fear the night
but despise sunlight,

don't call me
pet names
I will pick an ugly fight.

I'm no good at math
& have no patience,
I'm impossible to wake
& have zero motivation.

I believe in God
but have close to no morals,
I'm scared of ghosts
but addicted to the paranormal.

I don't want to be touched
on my face nor my hair,
I would choose **my** freedom
any day over being a millionaire.

I cannot sit
through a
fucking musical,
I can't keep a job
because I act
like a juvenile.

I'm banned from Best Buy
because that Samsung
guy sucks,
kissed the wrong member
of my favorite band,
just my luck.

I hate stuffed animals
& Valentine's chocolate,
I never trust anything
presented as flawless.

I hate the **way**
the government
is run today,

I'm surprised
I still haven't turned
all the way gay.

I'm not good
at relationships
or wanting a man,
I tell anybody
who wants me,
"Keep up if you can."

I Talk

To the Devil

In My Sleep

That's Why

The Angels

Wake Me

Rogue Planet

I recede into
the dark corners
past the martyrs
of the Cosmos,
back myself away
from the light
I used to dream
about at night,
rarely peeking into reality
from my
existential comatose.

Tomorrow's dance
was intimately ceased
in yesterday's orbit,
my celestial family,
I've given all I **have**,
I'm a Rogue Planet
whose gravity is
too weary to commit.

The planets
align to their
God-given **light**,
I observe
like a ghost
in a chapel,
there is no structure
for a maladroit
like me in hind-sight.

It's a lonely notion
finding my place
in these stars,
I plead with guilt;
this is just
what I need,
the Universe
is ever-expanding
I could never
be too far.

Empty Stage

City lights &
showered **storms**,
less we see
the sounds
are more.

To rid me
of this
ruthless chain,
take me away
& I'll take blame.

Sometimes
I can't feel a thing,
you bury me
with your **silent** shouting.

If this liquor
shall burden
me to life,

then death
is deemed
a drunken fight.

How could this curse
be a blessing,
for this game
I'll be first of ending.

Take my thoughts
& better days,
leave me
with this
forbidden shame.

When the whole world
waits to watch me,
they'll finally see
my stage is empty.

Homesick

How jealous

I am that you

are up there,

looking down

at us in **your**

heavy-duty gear.

Your mind

has forever

changed its priorities,

while we're still

beneath arguing

over superiority.

You start

your day with

hanging from a wall,

some of us

are **still** out

from last night

having a ball.

Tell me,

how does the Earth

look this morning

dear astronaut?

I bet

in that silence

you can't run

from any of

your thoughts.

Have all

the Amazon trees

fully disappeared?

Does 'Trash Island'

have a settlement flag

hanging off it's pier?

Have the wars

on Earth

stitched nuclear patches?

Do the bombs

to you resemble

a small book of matches?

I bet

from above

those worries are

miniscule anyway,

Or maybe

front row seats

would drive a sinner

to church

every Sunday.

I guess

what I'm trying to ask,

& I'll be quick,

is dear astronaut,

do you ever

get **homesick**?

Valentines' Day

I'm not one
for waiting on
Cupid all year,
I will not
light those candles
to create
that atmosphere.

I'm not the Scrooge
of Valentine's Day per se,
I just hate pink
& these hearts
are cliché.

I did however
make this holiday
my bitch once,
got through
the whole day
without fucking it up.

I dressed to kill
& went to the spa,
finally had an excuse
to wear
that sexy bra.

I went
to my favorite restaurant
& watched a
horror movie,
took my Glock
to the range &
practiced my **shooting**.

I saw my therapist
& she knew
something was up,
I went out
dancing alone &
for once I had fun.

My alarm
was set
to go off
every hour,
I texted myself
a compliment
each time
to practice self-power.

Drove home alone
& felt different
all night,
it was then
I decided
to stop feeding
my mental parasite.

Seeing as
I didn't want to

spend that day

on my knees,

I decided to date myself

exactly the way

I wanted it to be.

I imagined

everyone for one day

using that technique,

what if for one day

all our **imperfections**

were cured

with self-acceptance?

Voodoo Doll

I saw the way

you looked at yourself

through the mirror

last night,

it haunts me now;

that's not how

I remember you

in a fight.

I wish I could

put a blue band-aid

on **your** heart,

it could cover

the scabs you have

as you pick

yourself apart.

I'd wrap your bruises

in silk &

lay you in

my bed,

I could scream

louder than those

demons in your head.

I could

make a voodoo doll

of you & brush its hair,

put its hand

on its heart

to remind it of

something in there.

I would clean it

everyday

in my holy water &

hold it every night,

keep it warm

to expel

its internal

frost-bite.

Maybe then

your **mirror**

wouldn't be

a painful view,

I could heal

with this voodoo doll

I'd have of you.

I found out

you hated me

that I'm not good,

at least

we have something

in common

I hate me too.

Money

You all know
my name
& chase me
'til your death,
I've already
owned you since
your very first breath.

I control various lives
from Chicago's hookers
to the UK's Queen,
I'm what you
think of all day,
the All-Powerful Green.

I take the best
of people &
turn them to their worst,
I favor those
who **always**
put me first.

I've made the evil
genius rise &
control all your minds,
I've left good people
with nothing,
left them all behind.
I put **value**
in the nonsense
you're buying,
I've turned the coward
into today's
known lion.
I've made the
strongest women
bow down with submission,
to give their power
up in **my** name,
destroying their intuition.

I've brutally conquered
more division
than the seas,
I'm the mask
on your face
people wish to see.

You think
I'm a coach
but I'm a referee,
I'll cause more **chaos**,
the more you
disrespect me.

I've felt the magic &

seen the dangers

of this world.

What can I

really do?

I can be

magically dangerous too.

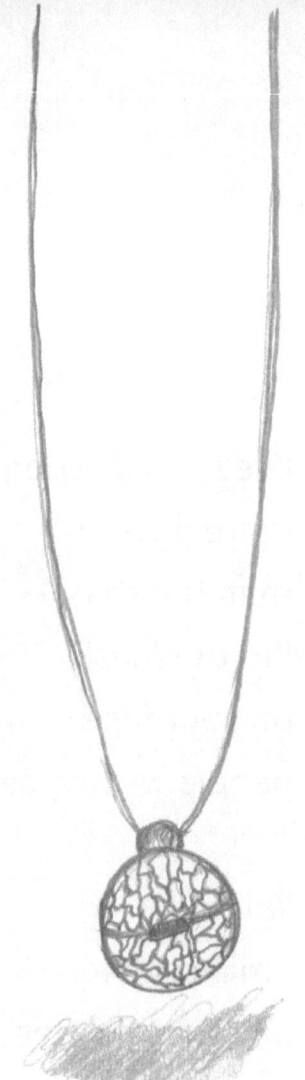

Transparency

Last night
in bed
when I was falling asleep
in my room,
I saw another version
of myself
getting into
my bed too.

She looked at me
with hunger swelled
in her eyes,
she didn't say much
but I **could** tell
she wanted to switch
me lives.

This morning
I woke up &
thought about her,

I began to

picture my life &

considered the offer.

How hard could it be

to **be** everything

I'm not,

I'm sure I could enjoy

being someone

else a lot.

I could use manners

at the dinner table,

be polite to your friends

& act presentable.

Charm your parents

with homemade pie

on the holidays,

solve all the
crossword puzzles
in the **boring** paper
every Sunday.

I could have babies
& hold them all day,
kiss my husband
goodbye before work
in the driveway.

I could sing
to my babies
& watch them fall asleep,
every summer brew
lemon strawberry iced tea.

Wear a dress
everyday &

paint my nails red,
maybe even have
just one sip of wine
only before bed.

I could cover my skin
& find fear of needles,
shock my brain
with electricity
& learn to be **simple**.

I could be someone
who wears sweaters,
let everybody know
I'm a home-maker,
not a wrecker.

What comes after
I change everything

about me?

Will I have purified
the water
inside my sea?
Will my blood
have ridden
all my toxicities?

Would my brain
find common ground
between polarities?

Would my skin repair
all the damage
I've done?
Would the ghosts
in my head
go from 28 down
to none?

I'm sure
I could find

all my old enemies
& win them
all over,
even after all this,
I know I'd go
straight back
to being a loner.

These words

will tell you

more than

I ever could,

I can advise

you not to read,

I don't know

if you should.

Shooting Star

Take me away
so my soul
returns **to** space,
this place is crowded
& seems to only
fall from grace.

Where I will fly
by **the** storm
of the Nebulae Eye,
instead of wasting
my days watching
the world go by.

The **stars** & I
have more in common,
than **you & me,**
as people are happy
to know when
I'm falling.

Stardust to radiation

I **will** become,

recycling my thoughts

in these galaxies

I become so lost.

The future,

past &

present tense,

all circle around

me & for once

it seems

to makes sense.

If there is a Heaven

I know mine will be there,

my kingdom is endless,

we'll **always** have

enough to **share.**

The planets

are my family

& is this

galactic life,

I have it all

in my hands,

such a beautiful sight.

My life

would be perfect

as a shiny star,

kids wishing on me,

reminding them

hope isn't too far.

Scientists below try

to figure me out,

try to learn all my secrets

as I mystify their doubts.

But here on Earth

I am to create

the best out of this,

I essence

the Universe,

in my heart will

remain its bliss.

Dangerous

Danger to me
is something **I** greet
when I feel nothing,
like meeting
an old friend;
it knows when
I'm coming.

It leads me
down a path
you **couldn't** direct me,
adrenaline pumping,
daring me
to compete.

Will I regret
the decisions
I **make** & find my debt?

Not backing down
to a game of Russian Roulette.

Apathy giving
no fucks
if I'm awake,
like that time
I got into a stranger's car
& we drove 800 miles away.

I wanted to fear

something but

ended up liking it,

knowing that any moment

this stranger's trust

I bought,

could've been counterfeit.

Or that time

I slithered out a

two-story window

to escape a demon,

Unfortunately,

I was caught in the arms

of someone

instead of falling free then.

I wanted to control

something that was

out of my reach,

drinking the poison

but immune to the bleach.

The most dangerous

place I'd been though

was in the mirror,

naked &

completely honest

with **myself** to

see a little clearer.

My eyes gone

completely black

& void of light,

blood pouring

from my mouth,

my tongue

had taken a bite.

Six ecstasy pills in to jump rope

with my lifeline,

that was a time

even the sun

couldn't make me shine.

I fear now

I might see another day

without it seeing me,

one of these days

someone might just **stop** me.

Karen

Came close

to the edge again,

running with shadows &

her ghost

in my head.

While **she** screams,

I feel another rip,

my ribcage

bruised from taking

all her hits.

I don't believe

in silence

because the quiet

screams out truth,

I make believe

these pills

help **me**

forget about you.

"Why so sad, my friend?"
Some dare to ask,
'sad' is just
a drop in the ocean's
deep vast.

I'm known to pursue
the running & numbing,
these pages
are all
I'm confronting.

I'm sewing
my lips
from speaking,
maybe then,
you'll only burden me
when I'm dreaming.

Wise grapes
from a vine
used as a liquid
lidocaine bottle,
what keeps me
in check is my
inner Aristotle.

With my tempest heart
& my two jagged feet,
I've running
out of places & people
to feel synthetically complete.

What a mess
I've made by
just being me,
I'm haunted by her
& she won't stop
fucking with me.

Astral

I constantly
reside in two
different realities,
one of the day-time
& one when I lay
me down to sleep.

I work
& pay bills
all to get older,
shallow minds
surround me
but I'm just a deep loner.

Everybody lies
& competes
to get ahead,
this continues from birth,
all the way to your **death**.

Where your body
is valued
above your mind,
we all seek
unnatural assets
to have a chance
to comply.

At night
I pray when
I crawl into bed,
for Michael to stay
with me as
I walk with the dead.

Each night is different
but that's what I crave,
when I open my eyes
in the land past the **graves**.

If I'm not spending time
with the ones
that I love,
I'm in another dimension
fighting to bring peace
from above.

The ankh in my skin
is from the night
I once fought,
the night the sky split
apart & the war
became onslaught.

I mediate each day
& I'm not to pick a side,
the two worlds
I know
will never collide.

Glimpse

I caught a glimpse

of a sad little girl,

made me wonder

what happened

to her world.

Maybe she felt

a little too deep,

maybe all her problems

were just on repeat.

Her face was of

a **broken** angel,

maybe her wings

held all her labels.

Faded halo

just above

her pretty face,

maybe she swam

in the devil's lake,

instead of

just having a taste.

I may have seen

some sweetness in her

but I can't tell,

because that glimpse

of her was

a **reflection** of myself.

Damned

"Going to Hell,"

she said,

"I'll be back again

tomorrow."

Tar in her veins,

shot of whiskey

for the sorrow.

Her **secrets** are written

all over her skin,

while everybody

stares & points

out the situations

she's been in.

Out-casted by love

she's **inflicted** with pain,

sin in her eyes

while angels weep

for her **in vain**.

Fire in Water
I'm burned out.
I write my story
from **fire**,
Sagittarius
the definition of haywire.
I've been around the Earth
& so much more,
it's isolating
to be awake
in the unconscious **war**.

Maybe Jupiter has
the same issues
but far away from me,
you'd do the same
if you were sewn
apart completely.

Here I incubate
in the depths

of the opposite,

we **together**

are the watery

fire-pit.

The world outside

has fallen away,

I'm daydreamed

in the minds of my

admirers' emotional fore-**play**.

I've learned to

shake out the

tragedy inside for now,

a digital bath

to keep me

six feet above ground.

Finish Line
What's the cure
when you're
your own disorder?

Falling asleep
conscious but waking up
in the same day
all over.

I meant it
when I said
I'll get up & **find**
help again,
it used to be
more fun when
I liked drugs back then.

The Pastor said
I need a lot more
than a 'Hail Mary,'

but I have found

an alternative **salvation**

in a library.

The psychic said

I'm **in** touch

with the Spirit World

so just take a breath,

the nurse

wants me on Lithium &

I just want to

survive my own head.

my therapist says

I'm lost in some

old trauma,

my suitors say

I just need to vacation

with them

in the Bahamas.

My shaman says

I'm sensing

too many things,

I went to the psychiatrist

& that bitch

still didn't believe me.

What would you do

if you played

in this game

of Cat & Mouse?

The dog-eat-dog world

right here

in your own house?

I think I've tried
it all & still
have no cure,
I find I'm **healthier**
staying away
from the dramas
of this world.

After all this,
I know it's
not for nothing,
pain is
my best teacher
& I ask it
to keep coming.

I can sit

here & say

to go through it

not over it,

when I make it

to the finish line,

I know

I won't be choking.

You told me

that day

you couldn't

see colours,

so I turned

around & gave you

my favorite

paint brush.

Bermuda Triangle

Do not come

for me

when **I** go missing,

or **change** your mind

away from unforgiving.

My heart is

the Bermuda Triangle

where Atlantis once lay,

you will see

the vacancy

through my abandoned

eyes some days.

The **dimensions**

in me are

warped & mortified,

I will suck you in

& leave you dry.

A lifetime

spent running

from those like you,

not knowing

I could collapse

& disappear

one day too.

God's Carousel

The corners

of the world

couldn't stop me

from the other side,

I've seen it

again in my head

spinning around the **light**.

I looked

at myself **&**

saw all of you

that night,

I met a different

reality & shook

the hand of time.

"Only few souls

have been there,

almost none come back," she said.

The time God

showed me

his hiding place

& **live** to

tell all of man.

Unimaginable thrill

that I might be

going home;

I didn't want to come back,

death was scared

of me because

I've seen its eyes

playing my soundtrack.

Open your mind

& your heart

is what I can

say for now,

the truth is here

& the only boundaries

are the ones you allow.

People come

& go

care not

what they think,

I've been this way

my whole life,

you can ask

all my shrinks.

One thing is certain

that I must clear up,

illusion is the problem

between all of us.

When you're done

with unaware

mortality,

find me;

I'll share with you

the corner

of my galaxy.

She asked me

if I've refrained

from violence

these days,

I said, "of course."

I've been teaching

myself to play drums

so I can beat the shit

out of something

without feeling

remorse.

Millennials
I'm so fucking
sick of these
children today,
turn off
your phone &
get outside
to play.

I don't blame
you for your
need of attention,
your parents
raised you
through their
own self-obsession.

Read a book
& try **to** sing,
try to **remember**
the best things
in life are free.

Sleeping on couches
& living on
welfare,
the rich
keep taking
when there's **nothing**
else to share.

Rapists in office
& uneducated chairman,
take all your rights
because your laziness
was predetermined.

Somewhere we lost
our raw intuition,
sold it all away
to the evil men
in business.

Guilty **is**
charged to
any **free**-thinker,
threat to society
you'll be if
intelligence lingers.

They poison
our water
& pollute our sky,
to keep us
sick & our
third eyes blind.

When the trees
are all gone &
animals have
been forgotten,

the greedy men
smile as the Earth
begins to rot.

Evolution of man
was supposed
to be a gift,
we are the disease
no planet
can rehabilitate.

Would you want
this future
for your kids to
see?
Knowing that a
change could have
started with me.

That Boy
Let's talk
about the boy
all the girls like,
charismatic charm
& his soft
dreamy eyes.

I'm watching
these girls like
how I watch
the Animal Planet,
mating season
never ends when
a woman's got to have it.

Lipstick & perfume,
these **women**
have no limits,
this boy is a walking
female mammal exhibit.

I begin to wonder

about the

social food chain,

about how high school

must be **stuck**

in some people's brains.

My humor takes off

in this comic book

roll & it's free,

then remember

how **high school**

just wasn't for me.

I've never once

competed with girls

for a man,

I have more

in common

with my words

than you ever can.

I wish

more women

knew their own worth,

Self-Empowerment

won't leave you

forever with

all this hurt.

This boy that I know

is an example

of our society,

I wish I we could

all wake up

together & finally see.

If alcohol

could talk

it would still

talk about you,

& about how I spent

too many nights

hugging a toilet

instead of you.

Visiting Hours: 3AM

The ageless group
stays curious,
young only means
new to
the **experience**.

25 & I'm barely
learning to speak,
about the man
from yesterday
& the person
I'll be next week.

My teens were angsty
& childhood was
close to non-existent,
my early 20's
were robbed by fear
& I grew distant.

What if

I told you

by now

I should have

been dead?

You wouldn't believe me;

you've never been

inside my head.

I'm a quarter life old

& still

have no talent,

I spent a year

studying Zen

to learn about balance.

I write because

I'm a visitor

in my **own** mind,

my brain

has language

even I

can't define.

Few have stumbled

upon my words

& I catch a

glimpse of their face,

my perspective

is addictive

& I dare it not

test your faith.

I only hope

the me tomorrow

will recover

lost youth,

find closeness

to those whom

I've withdrew.

Who lives

in the angst

but understands

the **pain,**

maybe finds

comfort in

being insane.

Jezebel

I've encountered

her lust before

maybe once or twice,

she gained my control

& commanded with

her seductive eyes.

Jezebel used my body;

I **tasted** her

deceitful powers,

the morning came

& she won all

those selfish hours.

I see her now

embodied in our

egotistical society,

the vanity gains

& she vexes

our sobrieties.

She preys

on the weak

our conceited **world**

is at stake,

self-deprecation

can feed our

narcissistic ways.

She lies **&** takes,

you'll never ask

why in captivity,

she owns the media

& mocks all of humanity.

She'll wane

on your spirit

as you forfeit

your heart,

you'll beg her

for **more**

as she tears

you apart.

I have a big

hole in my

world & I'm sorry

for letting you

think you could

fill it.

There's a boy
from **my** hometown
named Matt,
from grade school
all night & day
we would chat.

My first kiss ever
boy your **lips**
were cherry,
piece of me
died when I found
your name
in the obituary.

A pretty-faced girl,
who everybody knew,
it's been
some years
but I still smell you.

We laughed

all night &

shared our blues,

you liked me

but everybody else

loved you too.

There's a man

down south

I turn submissive

when he touches me,

we **wanted**

the future

& to marry.

He wanted to

give me the world

& that was so tempting,

all I had to do

was change

everything about me.

There's a guy

downtown holding

some years of mine,

sitting with a beer

& looking really fine,

could have made it

'til we were 80,

but I guess

I'm better at

reckless living

& self-shaming.

I thought

I did it all

'til y'all

let me in,

I fell too hard

but ran away

as I felt my **tears**

come creeping in.

They said

what we were doing

was a sin,

I'm bad at love

& that's just

the beginning.

Fixed

We've all heard
stories about that
"one girl,"
spreading her magic
around town
usually in a blur.

Seeing one side
of her story;
her friends
they all speak,
trying to keep up
with her tragedy
every damn week.

People around
are friendly to her face,

waiting to whisper
ancient words only
as she walks away.

She hides behind
mascara & a fake
smile today,
the smiling lips
of her friends
reek of unfriendly decay.

They dare not ask
of what takes place
in her nights,
creating scenarios
with invalid words
half-right.

The word fitting
to describe her
is "easy,"
while her boss
sends her home
for not dressing
up sleazy.

They consider
all options
regarding her past-list,
unaware this list
was predominantly
non-consensual hits.

The child beneath
this woman's explored skin,
was a previous vessel
for predatory grins.

Mommy was insecure
& craved attention
from men,
men loved the little girl
when she was only ten.
So the girl grew up
inside of her room
& filled out a figure.

Unsure if these
fantasies are normal
so she's silent,
they linger.

Learning late
how women can **be**,
it's as if
the humans
she attracts are untrustworthy.

Those men
she trusted
as an innocent child,
grew fangs
& dammed her
light away.
She's alone and exiled.
she lives as an adult
today paying bills
& catching some sleep,
wanting a friend around,
she needs a mental retreat.

The men throw their
hands up her skirt
grabbing a thigh,
she slaps him
& shouts
"Get out & Good-Bye!"

Every year
is different
there's always
a new man,
she desperately
desires for a female
to be her friend.

She thinks women
operate differently
amongst themselves,
she hopes
this one will last
without taking off a belt.

The judgement
she faces from her
soft-skinned new peer,

attraction to

the same sex is

but only to be **a** queer.

Truth is-first one

on the past-list

was in fact a female,

predators,

let me tell you

are not always

just males.

Her first **memory**

of saying "ouch" down there,

was the soft-skinned girl

knowing too much

about skin when its bare.

4 years old,
robbed by a girl
before a man,
maybe things
would have been differently
if back then
she had a dad.

Maybe it all stuck
with her subconsciously,
she empties herself
out **to** keep
everybody else happy.

All those involved
out there know who they are,
they've fed shame
into the little girl
within this woman's heart.

Hypocrite

It's true
what they say;
what stays
in your head,
controlling your life
when you've tried
hard to forget.

What got us ignored
& gave us attention,
designing ourselves
to desirable
spared affection.

To read a book
was rewarded
with ignorance,
failing a class
gave volume
to the hypocrites.

I'd brush my hair

because you adored

the length,

then cut it all off

just to spite

your name.

I would find

your cocaine

in various places,

then you'd burn me

at the stake

when you heard

of my first kiss.

You'd leave me

with strangers

to go on a binge,

you'd strike my face

for not moving fast

as I pack up

my things.

You yelled

& screamed

always cursing me out,

for not having

a voice &

shutting you out.

I'm a reactive adult

so I guess you

have the hand that wins,

my **secretive** face

knows your hand

also leaves a **sting**.

The ego
protects the Spirit.
At least society
is using SOME KIND
of protection.

Paradox

Leave me in bed,

I've locked

all the doors,

I'm not feeling well;

I'm dying to be bored.

Hide all the liquor

& leave on a light,

while my daytime

nightmares

accompany my mind.

You threw away

my scissors

like the time before,

we'll **wait** it

all out again,

because I'm sore.

To cry

is to be left

with another Prozac,

give me another

as my hair

gets tied back.

For another three months

I'll lay here

& bleed,

not enough meds

to make **me**

stop screaming.

Give me

a Lithium

& wait as

I vegetate,

to paralyze

my mind is

also for me

to not complain.

Life will go on

for everyone

I know,

I'll still be here

asking God

how my **brain**

become this broken.

Thoughtless **ghosts**
from her past
were fought
in the arms of his,
he had no power
or shields of gold
but felt her sorrow
through all this.

Her body is sore
but her fists
are still strong,
feels like they've
waited a decade
too long.

Who are they
& what are we?

Which compounds
will today ask
to feel complete?
Strung out
on the bed
of a hotel,
lies on their lips
but truth
hanging on a belt.

Maybe **society**
needs them dead
for this century,
locking lips
& facing the penalty.

They now haunt
the reflections
of their sins,

stones casted

at them

are collected

from those

faceless grins.

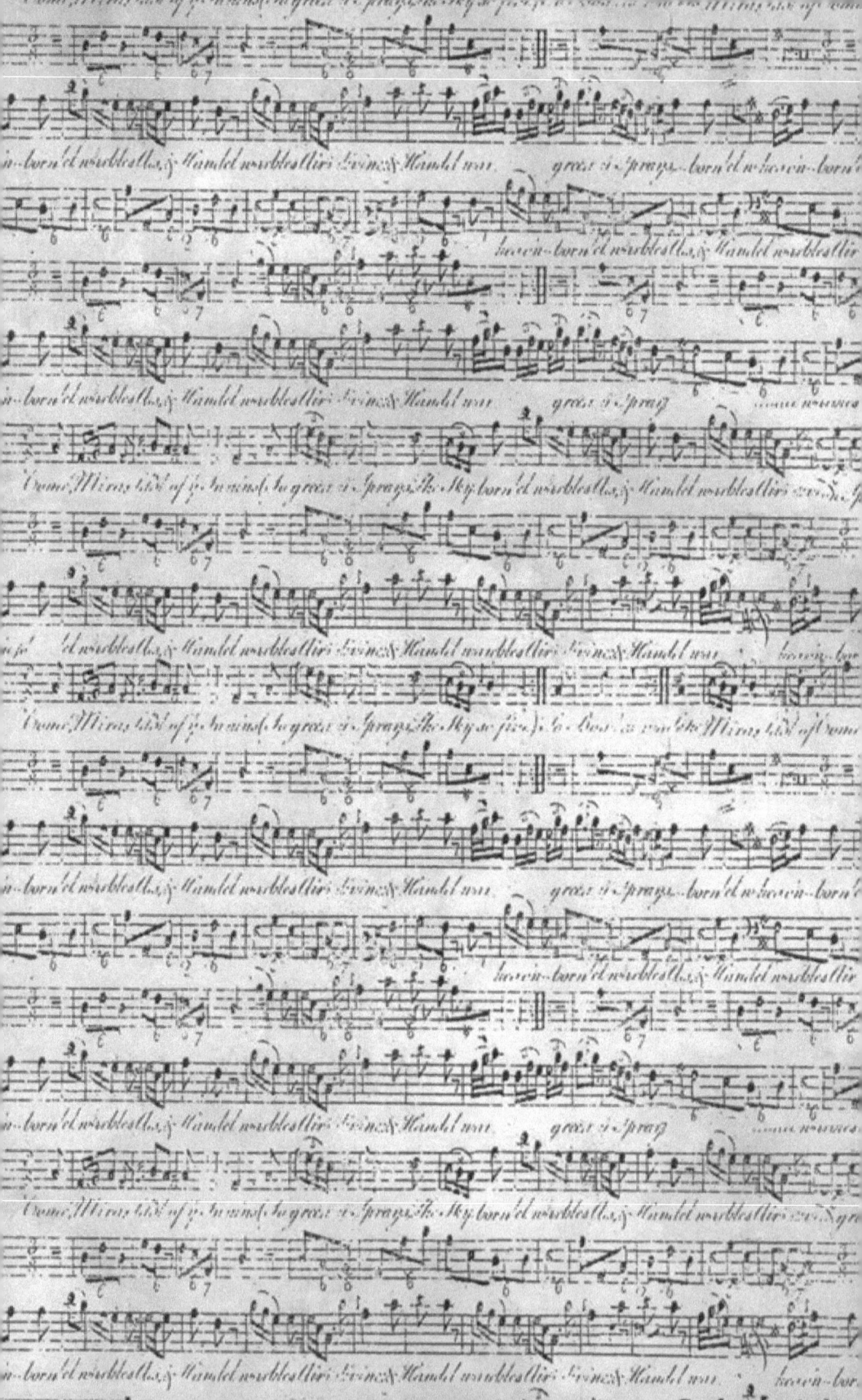

Camillo

You met me

for a moment

& I've known

you forever,

embracing your presence

was the hardest

to endeavor.

I shiver

at the sound

of **your**

seductive voice,

retaining my

composure, I pretend

I have poise.

I may only

be a face

in the crowd,

but to **me**

you're the only face

I'd like to have around.

Your pain, love

& anger is

what you

gave this world,

helped resurrect

the life of this

troubled girl.

You speak

in tones with

puzzling metaphors,

communication with

those like you

is all you're

looking for.

I'll never be

able to show

you my

entire gratitude,

for my next

hundred years

I will be honoring you.

Call me

the Mona Lisa

because when the

whole world is

watching me,

all I see is you.

Y Chromosome

I never
got the chance
to see **you** or
meet you,
the chance
to wonder if
I ever **wanted**
to be you.

I engage my time
to find you
one day,
usually wondering
if you're behind me
but won't ever say.

Did you ever
think of me or wonder
where I could **be**?

Nights as a kid
wishing I could run
with you
& be free.

I learn **alone**
everyday how
to fix myself,
do you have
secrets in life or
do you
disengage yourself?

I spend my time
wondering who
you are,
I usually have faith
you are never too far.

Would you be

proud of me

for rejecting love?

Would you sit

me down,

make **me** face

the truth from above?

Would you be

the one to give me

away on my Wedding Day?

Would you hate me

if I told you

I was gay?

You're the first man

to break my heart,

I'm grown up now
& don't need
a man to fall apart.

I hate you
& love you
but I'm sure
you do **too,**
give me a chance,
worst outcome is
I might like you.

Everybody kills

to be wanted,

but I've learned

it's lonelier

to have everyone

fall for you.

Intimacy only

makes me

more isolated.

Manic Me
Thanks
for knowing me
to anyone
reading this,
I've either
ruined your life
or left you
with a kiss.

I've probably
disgusted you
& made you
want to hurl,
or **made** you feel
like the most
important person
in the world.

I cannot say
how it all
started this way,

or when it

climbed inside me

& to come out

sometimes & play.

I'm sure

your favorite **Reese**

was the 'Manic Me',

the Reese

that threw parties

& never went to sleep.

The popular Reese

who's been adored

by the town,

but she always

knew just how

to **burn** the

whole city down.

The shameless Reese

who took off

her clothes,

the wild demon

in me possessing

my **bones**.

I've watched

'Manic Me'

from behind

the scenes,

praying to be small

& dared not

to be seen.

When the

come down came

& the parties

all end,

that demon

vacated &

took all my friends.

Left me here
with these memories
I do not want,
feeling as empty
as all this useless
shit she bought.

To whom

it may concern,

I ask

that you forgive,

my self-punishment

is the recollection

of you

to forever relive.

WWIII

I've made amends

with who

I used to **be**,

the girl

who drank a bottle

& set fire

to money.

Who ripped up

her poems

& scarred up

her walls,

unforgivably cracked

her best friend's jaw.

She hated herself

& kicked out her mirrors,

cursed out to God

& finished all the liquor.

Put a light

to her pipe

to drown out

her demons,

the smoke pressed her

silence but

also quieted me.

I always had faith

she would hear

me one day,

I'm the wildfire

in her even at times

when I was only **a** flame.

She survived her own war

so I'm **patient** with her,

WWIII is internal

& YOU are a **survivor.**

About the Author

Reese O'Connell was born in December 1993 in Albuquerque, New Mexico to a single mother as a fifth child. At the age of 5, her family moved to New York where she was raised with her siblings to a self-sacrificing grandmother and dedicated uncle. She had a happy childhood but never felt like she was in the right place with the right people. At 15, Reese moved to Texas to start a new life and find herself. She spent another 10 years in Texas evolving how she wanted to live her life. Although Reese dropped out of high school, she worked hard at her jobs including bartending, book-selling, and running coffee shops. Reese battles with a sometimes crippling mental disorder and works hard at keeping herself together through working, writing and her love of Astronomy. She holds high regard for the people in her life that stuck around in her most hopeless moments of her life including her uncle, grandmother and adoptive family. After much relocation, Reese now happily resides in Louisville, Kentucky.

www.ingramcontent.com/pod-product-compliance
Lightning Source LLC
Chambersburg PA
CBHW030856170426
43193CB00009BA/628